THE HEART

OF

A

HUSTLER

"A MAN TRANSFORMED"

MICHEAL "PISTOL" MONROE

Divinely Inspired Publishers

Fayetteville, NC

The Heart of a Hustler

Copyright © 2017 Micheal Monroe

ISBN-13: 978-1978074842

ISBN-10: 1978074840

Email: kingdombiz23@aol.com

This book is intended to tell the story that was once untold, but now has been told. To display the beginning of a Transformational process in my journey to becoming SOLD OUT to God!

Micheal Monroe

✝ DEDICATION ✝

I would like to dedicate this book to my mother the late great Eula Denise Monroe, the one that truly taught me how to hustle. To my kids and to everyone that paved the way for me. To everyone in Robin Heights, and the entire Bucktown! We made it and no one can take that from us!

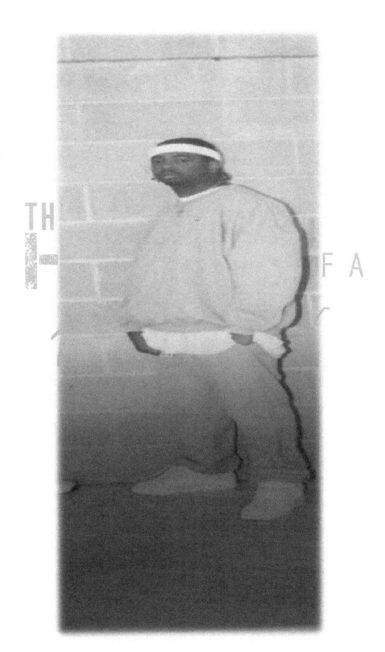

The Beginning:

This is how it all started, I remember growing up back in the late 1980's early 90's around hustlers and drug dealers all my life. Back when the movie New Jack City first came out. I was so fascinated by the character Nino Brown. I remember telling my mom that I wanted to be a drug dealer, but in movies because I didn't want to go to jail. The reality was I was afraid of going to jail, but I was infatuated with the lifestyle of being a drug dealer. My mom grew up in the mean streets of Baltimore Maryland, and as a little girl she used to go around the city to collect people's bets because my great-grandmother was a number runner throughout the city. I used to hear all the stories about how my mother used to go to collect the bets and keep the money in her socks to keep from getting robbed by all the neighborhood predators. My aunt's husband was a close friend of Little Melvin, so therefore my mom was exposed to a lot of the Gangsta side of the city and the boosting, prostitution, gambling; you know and the heroine selling that was going on in the city. But in her early 20's, she decided to pick up and move down south to North Carolina to live with one of her aunts. It was there that my mom found herself in a lane all by herself being that she was a lot more advanced than the average woman in the small town that she was now living in. My mother was a natural born Hustler. A lot of people don't know that my mom bought her first car picking up cans. I can remember being as young as two years old walking up and down the street with my mom picking up cans. Then at a young age, my mom decided to open up her own juke joint in the area, while working at one of the local factories. My mother also sold weed to a lot of people throughout the town which was another way that I gained so much popularity. I can remember getting up early on Saturday mornings and riding over to Fayetteville to paradise records in order to buy records to go inside the jukebox at the club. I was also given the task of cleaning up the club on Saturday and Sunday mornings after everyone had finished partying. From day one, my mother taught me the value of a dollar and the means of Hustling to get it. I used to watch my mother sit at the kitchen table and cut and bag up weed at least 3 to 4 times a week. That's where I made a promise to my mother and to myself that I would never smoke it and until this day I never have. It's funny because even though my mother had money, she used to drive some of the Raggediest cars. I mean, I used to hate for my mother to take or pick me up from school. I was afraid all my friends were going to laugh at me. It was good during those early years, you know being that my mom had so many hustles going on. She was able to buy me all the nice shoes and clothes and things of that nature. I can remember wearing those sweaters that Bill Cosby used to wear on the Cosby show and everybody talking about how nice they were. I can remember getting my first pair of Jordan's when I was in the fourth grade, at that time my friend Brent and I were the only ones that had a pair. But over the course of time, my mother eventually brought my aunt and her kids down along with my grandmother and uncle which kind of limited our living space. What I was not aware of was that it would eventually result in me not being able to wear the nice clothes and shoes that I was accustomed to wearing. I kind of resented my cousins and my aunt living with us. Nevertheless, at the end of the day it was fun because I had someone to play with every day. My cousin Nana was my favorite. She was my little girl cousin and I believe, I was her idol or something, because she would follow me everywhere I went. We were kind of like business partners. It's crazy because we used to come up with all the different types of ways and schemes to make money. I can remember being around the age of eight years old and my mother and I took some trash to the trash dumpsters, and I found a box of metal close hangers and I took the box of hangers' home, and put the hangers in groups of 10 and began selling them in the neighborhood for a dollar a bundle. I remember my friends laughing at me because I was selling clothes hangers, but they just didn't know that it was the beginning to my career as a hustler. Then around age of ten, I began picking up bottles and cans and started my own recycling business right there in my backyard. It wasn't long before Nana joined me in my little endeavor and became my business partner. Shortly thereafter, my friend Wayne and I began raking yards throughout some of the white neighborhoods that surrounded the area where we lived. I remember going to the store and buying a pack of index cards and writing our business name and phone number on there and passing them out to different houses in the neighborhoods. One year for Christmas my mom asked me what I wanted for Christmas and I told her I wanted a lawnmower and she asked me why and I told her so I could cut grass and buy my own G.I. Joe men so I wouldn't have to ask her to buy them for me. So, I got a lawnmower for Christmas and started cutting grass throughout the neighborhood and of course everyone thought I was crazy for getting a lawnmower for Christmas, but I didn't care because I was making money! My early Hustling' days even took me all the way to Baltimore Maryland, where I used to stand on the street corners of busy intersections and squeegee car windows as they stopped at stop lights. Man, that had to be the funniest summer ever! I probably made around $800 within the course of five weeks. Nana was up there with me that summer so, I kind of felt like I had the responsibility of making sure she was taking care of while we were there. Whenever I used to come in from squeegeeing, we used to always go around to the carryout and buy chicken boxes and sunflower seeds. Things really got good when I went up Monument Street and purchase two of the squeegee's and got the other kids on the corner to start working for me. You know whatever they made from squeegeeing a window they paid me half for using my squeegee. I guess you can say that was my first experience in leveraging somebody else's time and energy. All important lessons that would prove to be valuable, once I entered the drug trade. I started selling drugs around the age of 15 or 16. I think I might've been in like the 10th grade. At first, I was scared because like I said before, I was afraid of going to jail. What happened, was a friend of mine who didn't grow up in the same circumstances that I grew up in or in the area that grew up in started selling. I was like what the heck! If he can do it, I know I can do it. I mean considering that I came from a rough neighborhood and was known to be a tough guy and he wasn't. I felt like that would make it easier for me to sell drugs than for him to do so. One day he brought some drugs to school, and showed them to me. I was just amazed by the fact that he was actually doing it. So, one afternoon I caught the bus to his house and he took me over to the drug spot where he bought his drugs from. I bought back then what we considered to be a five for fifty. It's crazy because the rocks were so big that you could actually bust them down in half and make two rocks out of one rock. So, that's how my drug career started. But the funny thing is I ended up getting beat out of all my crack. What happened was, one of my homeboys from a neighborhood told me he had a sale around the corner for three rocks. So, we went around there to make the sale. When we arrived there, I gave him the drugs. He went in the front door the of house and went out the back door and left me standing outside in the front yard. What I didn't know is that my homeboy, even though we were the same age he began smoking crack himself. Man, I was messed up because that was the money that my mom had given me to go to Baltimore that summer. I went to Baltimore that summer, but I lied and told my aunt that my mother didn't give me any spending money. During that time, Mobb Deep came out with the song "Survival of the Fittest." I used to listen to that song over and over again. I remember getting in trouble with my aunt, because I kept calling the "Box" and ordering that song. At that point, it was all about survival and I came back from Baltimore with the mindset that I was going to take over the world. When I arrived, I immediately began scoping the neighborhood to see who was who and what was what. Around that time, my man Rick and Richie practically had the whole hood on lock with the exception of a few dudes here and there that were making a few dollars. Those two guys were basically supplying the whole town, but I had plans to get a piece of the pie. Home from summer vacation and no money, how was I going to get started? Selling dummies (chipped off pieces of soap or anything else that resembled crack) was a big thing back then. It just so happened that Rick got locked up in Virginia and his girlfriend was now running his spot and it was free game. One night my cousin and I was there and a couple of sales came through. My cousin Shen was selling this guy a $20 rock and in the process of him doing that a white guy came wanting a slab ($100). So, I went in the bathroom where my cousin was and began cutting the slab off the bar of soap. My cousin Shen was like "man you can't cut it that big" and I said, "man he wants a slab" so, of course my cousin was mad because he missed out on a hundred-dollar sale. When I came out to serve the white guy, the guy that my cousin had just sold to, pulled back into the yard and yelled out "they're selling soap." So, the white guy turned around quick, but before you know it my cousin and I had already started running through the backyard to a path onto the next street over. With a fresh hundred and the money I already had in my pocket, I was ready to go and cop my own slab and hit the block. I immediately went to Rich and coped me a slab. At this point, I began living with my grandparents which made it a lot easier to maneuver being that they were older, and I had a little bit more freedom. Besides, they lived in Robin Heights and everybody knew that Robin Heights was the place to be. Back in those days, I didn't even know how to cut it up. I used to get my cousin Shen to do it for me, and of course he was hitting me in the head a little bit. I really didn't know any better at the time. One of the first times, I ever saw any crack was one weekend I stayed at my grandmother's house and went to school from there. Fortunately, I had a pair of sweatpants that I left there previously. So, I put those on and just got a shirt from one of my cousins. But when I got to school I reached in my pocket found about 4 small crack rocks. Man! I was so mad and disappointed. I immediately went to find Shen, and when I found him I said, "man look, what is this?" He was like "give me that". Apparently, he had worn my sweatpants and forgot he left them in the pocket. Now, that I think about it they probably were fake anyway. So, out on the block I quickly began learning the rules to the game and what it meant to be a hustler/drug dealer. Man, you learn a lot from the game that users try to run, as well as managing your own business. Back then it was nothing for me to stay out until 2 - 3 in the morning, sometimes all night hugging the block. It's crazy, I remember when I first started hustling, I went to all the older guys on the block and tried to get them to put our money together and form an organization, but because they were older and had been hustling a lot longer than me they weren't with it. As time went on, I gradually started seeing some of them dudes fall off, while I was gradually getting stronger and stronger. Eventually, I earned the respect of most of the older Kats in the hood and the dudes that sold weight started noticing my potential. My hustling game really got Richie's attention and he took me under his wing and started showing me the ropes. Richie was like one of my idols growing up along with Bubba Dee and Andre aka "Playboy" but regarding hustling to me Richie was a genius. Till this day, I'll tell anybody that when it came to hustling, Richie was a genius. Richie and I got tight around that time, and then we found out we were cousins on my father's side so, that just made it even better. Richie used to let me drive his rental cars around the hood, and to get something to eat from one of the local restaurants. It's crazy, because I used to always wait until it was time for school to let out to ask him to drive to Burger King or McDonald's so I could ride through by the high school. Man, those were days!! We used to play ball at the park for hours all the while waiting for smokers to come to the court, and buy a rock or two. Sometimes, Richie would leave to go to New York, he would come by the crib to make sure I was straight until he got back, and if I wasn't he would leave me a quarter or half ounce. Usually by time, he came back I had already sold it and had his money waiting for him. Things really got serious when I decided to ride up there with him, at one point to take his daughter home. The plan was to ride up there, and drop his daughter off and turn around to come back before anyone even realized I was gone. I mean, it was nothing for me to stay out all night every now and then. So, I figured I could get away with it without anyone finding out. Unfortunately, that wasn't the case. We left out like early that evening with the hopes of getting there that night and coming back early the next morning. Well the next morning, Richie's wife needed to use the van to go shopping or something. So, we decided to go play basketball around the corner while she was gone to kill time. Besides, I couldn't wait to show these New York Kats how we get down in Robin Heights. When we arrived at the court, it's a few guys out there hooping. So, Richie introduces me to the guys and was like this my little man from down south that I've telling y'all about. So, we picked teams and began playing and of course, I was busting their tales real good. Then out of nowhere a guy from Richie's building came running to the court screaming that Richie's wife had been in a wreck. We immediately left the court and caught a cab to the location of the accident. When we got there his wife is sitting on the curb crying. I mean the van is smashed up, but thank God, she was ok. What happened was she ran a red light, and smashed into some guy. The next few days proved to be real crazy. When Rich called the rental car place they said they wouldn't have any available until Monday. When he told me what they said, he asked me if I wanted to catch the bus home, but I said no. I figured a couple of days more wouldn't hurt. Besides, I was really scared because I had left without telling anyone where I was going. So, the turnaround trip ended up being like 5 days. After five days, we finally got word from the rental car service, that we could come and pick up another van. So, Rich and I took the train from the Bronx to Newark airport to pick it up. I remember that ride home like it was yesterday. All that was going through my mind was "what in the world am I going to tell my family once I got home". We got back in town around 6 o'clock that evening and I remember Richie dropping me off at the store. As soon as I got out of the van, my man Matt was like "where have you been? "Everybody been looking for you!!" I hung out for a second, then took that long walk home. When I arrived there, I walk in and everyone was sitting in the living room staring me in the face. I just sat there speechless until my grandmother asked me where I been. My reply was "I went to New York with Richie". Man! you should have seen the look on my grandmother's face. She was like "you went all the way to New York and you didn't tell nobody". "And the nerve to stay gone all week". I tried to explain what happened, but it was no use. I was just happy to get out there alive. So, that was the end of that, and Richie compensated me well for all the trouble I went through. The sad thing is, I missed the last week of school and ended up failing the eleventh grade that year. In November 1996, I ended up catching my first charge. That summer, I began talking to a young lady that happened to be real close to one of my cousins. So, one night I was walking my cousin and his friends home from the store because the neighborhood can get kind of crazy at night. Plus, I wanted to take the opportunity to get a little bit more information about ol' girl from myself as we walked. When got to his aunt's house we stood outside talking when a police cruiser rode by. Mind you, I'm dirty but I figured I was out of harms way being that I wasn't exactly in the worst part of the hood. So, a few minutes later the police cruiser came back, but this time he rode up on the curve. I tried to, but I couldn't move! It was as if my feet were glued to the ground. The police hopped out and said "Micheal Monroe, I have a warrant for your arrest!!" As he searched me he found the the 17 "crack rocks" I had hidden in my pocket. He took me to jail and charged me with possession with the intent to sell and deliver crack cocaine. I also found out that the original warrant was for a secret indictment. Apparently, I sold some crack to undercover officers in July of the same year. I was placed under a $10,000 bond. Being that I was only 17, I was placed in the juvenile cell where I stayed for the next 35 days, because my mother wanted to teach me a lesson. The first couple of days was rough, but after that the time started going by pretty easy. After 35 days, my mother finally decided to come get me on December 21, two days before my birthday. Man, that was the best birthday present ever! Back on the streets, I knew it wouldn't be long before I jumped back into the mix. After Christmas break was over, we went back to school and every one treated me like a celebrity. I could even hear the teachers whispering, as I walked down the hallway. But the fame, wouldn't last too long before I found myself into more trouble with the police. However, this time for assault on a government official, and resisting arrest which stemmed from a brawl, we had with the cops during a high school basketball game. With that incident along with a few suspensions, my mother advised me not to go back to school. Her logic was that they didn't want me out there any longer. That was right up my alley seeing as though, I hardly attended school on Fridays, or on the first and the third. The bus driver already knew not to stop at my house on the first and the third. With all that free time, I had no other choice but to get money. I could stay out as late as I wanted without having to worry about getting enough sleep for school the next morning. I found myself in and out of crack houses all times of the night. When I wasn't in the crack house they would come and tap on my window, and I would serve them through the hole that I put in my window screen.

The Come Up:

After I dropped outta school I ended up moving to Park Place with my aunt Diane and that's where I really blew up. I exploded in the hood, so I figured I would move to have a little change of scenery. The real reason was my girlfriend lived across the street in North

Raeford was that made it easier for me to spend time with her. I remember sneaking in her window to have sex and almost getting caught on a few occasions. It was cool because her mom used to let her and her little sister come to the crib. Little did she know, my aunt had violated her probation and was sent to prison for six months leaving me with a house all to myself at the age18. Even though, I had moved out of Robin Heights, I still went there mostly every day to hustle until I started hanging in Queenmore, real tough and started getting money over there. During my time in Park Place, I started selling weight. What happened was the boy Rick was getting hit off by this kid named Jay. But on the rea,l the boy Rick kept coming up short with the money. So, I told my man Bub to holla at Jay for me, but the boy Jay wasn't trying to hear it. Bub was like " I'm telling you, you need to holla at the boy Pistol, he's the one that really got the hood on smash. But Jay still wasn't trying to hear it. In the meantime, Rick and I put our money together and took a trip to DC to cop 4 and a half ounces of crack. When we got back Rick helped me cut a few grams and a few eight balls and the rest I cut up in dubs(20's). Rick sold his work in a couple of days. but I wasn't used to selling weight, so it took me a lot longer to get rid of what I had. So, after Rick had sold all, if someone wanted to buy some weight, he started sending them to me because he needed me to hurry up and sell out, so we could make another trip to DC to re-up. In the meantime, Rick started gambling and lost his re-up money. Then one day I saw the boy, Jay and I told him I needed to holla at him. So, he came to my house in Park Place and asked me what was up. I asked him how much would he charge me for 4 1/2 ounces of crack. His response was "$3500." I told him to let me give him $3000, and I give him the other $500 when made the money. He agreed and left and came back with the 4 1/2. I immediately broke the scale out and started bagging up grams and eight balls. By the end of the day, I had made the $500 I owed Jay plus some. I called him and told him to come get his money. He was like "already!!" I was like "man I don't play!!" Two days later, I told him to bring me another one. Two days after that I told him to bring me another one. Every time I told him to bring me another one his response was "you done already!" It wasn't that I was out, but my motto was to never run out. Whenever I got to my last ounce, I would call him to bring me another one so I wouldn't run out. That went one for a minute beginning around the first part of "97" up until I went to prison the following January.

The Queenmore Days

At this point, I was the only one in Raeford selling weight at the time. I was supplying the whole town at 18 years old. I had dudes from every neighborhood buying weight from me. I mean things were good. Back then if you wasn't buying weight from me you had to drive all the way out to South Hoke or different parts of Robeson County for drugs. The boys and I from Queenmore started hanging real tight so, it was quite naturally that dudes would eventually start coming over there looking for me which caused that spot to explode like crazy. Man, everybody in Queenmore was getting money. Every one had cars with rims and music. We stayed at the mall buying clothes and shoes. We thought we were No Limit for real! What we had in Queenmore is what I had envisioned for Robin Heights, but it never happened. We used to sit around and gamble all night long and trap. Man! we had so much artillery that we could have easily shutdown any neighborhood in America. We used to go the club every weekend, no matter where it was riding back to back!! Out-towners didn't stand a chance. We ran the city and went out of town and ran that town as well. When we walk in the clubs, everybody would say "Oh Lord there go them Buck-town niggas!!" The spot at the boarding house used be so sweet, because we had so many places to stash our drugs in the vacant rooms or the woods that surrounded it. When the police would come down the hill by Upchurch, the cars would whistle so we knew they were coming. On August 21, 1997 is the year I bought my first car, a 1991 Honda Accord. The crazy thing about it is, I got put on house arrest the next day for sixty days and was stuck in the house. So, here I am with a brand new car with a new set of Fat Boys on it, and I'm stuck in the house on house arrest. I had to come up with a plan. The next time I went to see my probation officer I told him I was working with my uncle raking straw and going to school at night to get my GED. Like a dummy, the officer fell for the lie, and I was allowed to be out of the house from 6 in the morning to 9 o'clock at night. Not bad for someone on intensive probation with a seven o'clock curfew. With all the free time, I rode around making deliveries to everyone that wanted to buy some crack and show off my car at the same time. Man, we were wild back then. It wasn't nothing for us to go the club and end up in a all out brawl or shootout! I remember one night we went to this club way in South Carolina. We were about three or four cars deep. We had a case of Ice houses in each car. Back then we used to say "we're going down plank" road because Ice House was our beer of choice. We were initially going to a club in Rockingham, but we ended up getting lost. So, we stopped at a store to get directions and everyone could take a piss. When we stopped to ask this guy for directions and he informed us that the club was closed on Friday's but everyone went to the Universal Lounge on Friday nights. I mean we didn't know where it was so, we followed him to the club. When we got there the club was empty, but we decided to go in anyway. On this particular night we had convinced the Big Homie "Wolf" to go with us. So, when we got out of the car to go in Wolf was like " man y'all taking the guns in?" We're like "man don't you see all that security at the door." Wolf was like " man they know me down here." I told him man don't nobody know your country behind tale. But he insisted that they did. So, we gave him the 357 and the 38. When we got to the door the bouncer was like "what up Big Tew." That was Wolf name that he earned while doing time in prison. I mean were all in shock and Wolf looked back at us like see nigga I told you!! So, for that matter he was the man the rest of the night. It was crazy because Wolf bought the bar out that night. We couldn't believe it because this nigga was tight. We were all lined up at the bar and Wolf sat by the cashier so, he could pay for the drinks. It's crazy. Whenever we got our drink, we would just go to the back of the line and come around again until we were all drunk. I'm telling you the club was so empty, we were on the dance floor breaking dancing. But that all changed around 1 o'clock. Before we knew it, the club was stacked wall to wall. Man, we had a good time. My girlfriend From Red Springs and her crew was down there and I began putting my homies on to her friends. Unfortunately, my man Reggie B ended up getting into a confrontation with some dude over one of her friends. While I was trying to defuse the situation, I could see dudes going around whispering in one another's ears. So, I went and told everybody to be on guard because it was about to go down. I told my girlfriend and her crew to go ahead and leave because it was about to get ugly. But you know we're "No Limit Soldiers" which meant we were highly trained for situations like this. We got back to back and made our way to the cars so we could strap up. The whole while we were looking for Wolf, he was in the car sleep with the 357 and the 38 tucked in the small of his back. Man, we had a time trying to roll that big joker over to get those guns. As we made our way to my car some dudes started shooting in the air as they were leaving. I immediately opened fire at them which caused as series of shots to go off. As I was shooting, I heard my girlfriend scream out my name. As I turned to look all I could see was gunshots coming from the car beside them. By this time, I was out of bullets. So, yelled and told my cousin to get the car where the shots were coming from. Man! you should have seen how he came up out of the backseat of the Honda with those two chrome nine Rugers. It was like something out of a movie. It's like I was watching it in slow motion. When he came up out of my backseat, he was dumping like crazy, but the bullets were hitting the ground. I was like "yo raise them joints up!" Man, I'm telling you, bullets were flying everywhere. At this point, it started drizzling. So, we jumped in the car and peeled out. Well my man girl jumped in the car with us. She was all crying and carrying on. I kept telling her to shut up so I could think, but she kept carrying on. Then she started screaming she had to go back. I was like " no you don't." She responded that she did, that she had some girls riding with her and she had the keys and held them up in my face. We did a bullet check, and all we had was one bullet left. Out of four guns, all we had was one bullet. I immediately pulled over and hopped out the car and jumped into the ditch. Mind you, it's raining and lots of strange cars are riding by. We just got into a shootout with God knows who, we don't know how to get home, and all we have is one bullet left. My first instinct was to get out of harms way. Once all the cars rode by, I got back into the car and turned around to take ol' girl back to her car. When I pulled up, the security guard threw a pump shotgun in my window. I was like "hold up big man we're just bringing this girl back. He was like what y'all doing shooting at us." Apparently, as were leaving one of the homies decided to bust a few shots at the security guards. So, we left, and ol' girl showed us how to get back to Raeford. What a close call, but we made it. And you know I called my girlfriend and cussed her out real good for being hard headed and not leaving when I told her to. This was before Reek and I started hanging, but he used to have his mother to bring him to my house in Park place to buy drugs. The way he got her to do it is, he told her that my girl worked at beeper store and that she was hooking him up. Man, we had Park place and Queenmore on fire at the time. It was nothing to sale an ounce or two in dubs a day. I was still on probation at the time, but what I would do is, if I had to leave I would have my little man from next-door and his girlfriend come sit at my house. However, if my probation officer came while I was gone, he would go in the bathroom, and turn on the shower and talk to my probation officer to the bathroom window. I also left him with work from time to time, so if I was gone and people needed to get straight; they could go by and see him. I was able to go out of town, and still make money at the same time. The summer of ninety - seven is when Bobby and I started hanging tight. Y'all remember the green Honda with the Fat Boys on it? We were playing Club Mingles real hard back then. Some kind of way, Bobby started beefing with some crips from over in Fayetteville. One night after the club, we were all parked at the Hardee's on Skibo and Raeford Rd. Bobby was at the store beside Hardee's getting gas when a car load of crip niggas pulled up on him and tried to rush him. I immediately ran through the bushes, and tossed him the .38 that I had tucked in my waistline. Bobby caught the gun by the handle, and started shooting at the crip dudes. In the meantime, one of the crips tried to jump in Bobby's car and drive off ,but my man Maurice stopped him in his tracks. They began shooting at one another driving up skibo road until one of Bobby's tires got shot out. Bobby then whipped the car around and sped back down Skibo Rd. My crew and I jumped in the car to go after him to make sure he was alright. We later caught up with him at the gas station across from Southgate. He pulled around the back of the store so he wouldn't be easily seen. We changed the tire and later meet up at my house to playback the events of that night. From that point, we were thick as thieves. He began hanging in Queenmore with us and it was on and popping. Eventually, we fell out over some guns and what not.

Blood Brothers:

Reek and I finally hooked up around the end of the year. He went to Seattle to live with his aunt, but after a short while of being there he was ready to come home. The only problem was he didn't have any money to catch the bus. He called me and told me his situation, and said he would pay me back as soon as he got straight. I asked him how much was the ticket and he was like $240, but he told not to worry about sending him money to eat with. I asked him how long was the ride and he was like a week. I told him I couldn't let him ride the bus for a week with no money to eat. So, I sent him like $300. When he got home, he came to the crib to thank me. I asked him was he ready to get paid. His response was "yeah what I gotta do." I told him the first thing he gotta do is stop smoking weed. The reason I told him that was because first I needed him to be focused, and secondly, I didn't want him supplying the party. See when you have money, dudes will smoke a blunt with you just to get you started. They know you're going to supply the weed for the rest of the night. But we didn't need that because we were trying save as much money as we could, so we could move up in the game. Besides, I wasn't trying to make another drug dealer Rich. If I learned anything from the Rick situation, it was no matter what; always keep your re-up money. Then there was that infamous night, we commonly refer to as the night that could have sent us away forever. We had completed several run ends with those crip dudes from Fayetteville. It just kept going back and forth from basketball games to clubs to run ends at the mall until finally we had done had enough. I think the last incident was when my man and I was in the club throwing up fake gang signs, when we got surrounded by a group of gang members. Just so happened one of the guys knew my cousin and asked me if I was Blood and I told him no. So, he turned around and told the guys that had surrounded us that we were not Bloods. So, they slowly turned and walked away with looks of disbelief. But as soon as they turned to walk away a incident popped off and people began running through the club. Just so happened, one of the leaders of the Gang accidentally dropped his gun right in front of me as he was running to address the situation. I immediately stepped on the gun and drugged it with my foot to a near by chair. I slowly eased down and picked the gun up and tucked it in my back pocket. I found my man and told him we were leaving, but he was skeptical because we didn't have a gun. I pulled the gun out of my pocket and showed it to him. He was like "where did you get that from?" I told him it fell out of ol' boy pocket. He grabbed the gun and was like "come on!" The dudes were so occupied with the other situation that they totally forgot about us. We hopped in the car and drove off. As a result, one Saturday evening we were contemplating what club we were going to that night. So, when the particular club was mentioned that these crips hung at it was if we go there we're not going in we're shooting it up. I was like cool that's where we're going. I tried to warn everyone I knew, including my girl and her friends that usually went there not to go on this particular night because something bad was going to happen out there. But no one listened. As midnight drew near, we went to the spot and loaded up making sure we didn't leave any fingerprints on any shell casings. We then made our way to Fayetteville with nothing, but thoughts of payback on our minds. We had this particular song that was like our theme song that was played wherever we went. As we approached the club, all we heard was multiple gun shots ring out and people screaming. As we proceeded to send a message to these Cats, that we weren't nothing to play with. As we sped off from the crime scene, we were racing through the streets of Fayetteville at very high speeds when we were approached by a State Trooper with his blue lights on. Scared to death, we began tossing the guns out of the windows. The plan was to shoot up the club, and then pass the guns off to another car that wasn't as recognizable. But that all changed as were being pursued by a State Trooper. My heart is racing as he gets closer, but all of sudden as he approaches the car, he then goes around us sped off out of sight. We all let out a sigh of relief, because we thought it was over for us. We made it safely back to the hood and went to the Barn to give ourselves a alibi, just in case the cops came wanting to know our whereabouts. Finally, I ended up violating my probation and going to prison in January of 1998. I served 7 months for possession with the intent to sell and deliver "crack" cocaine. It was like being at a summer camp for boys. I actually had a good time.

All we did was play basketball and dig around and talk about girls. I was right down the road from my house at Sandhills Youth Center, so my homeboys would ride through the parking lot and holla at me from time to time. Serving the 7 months placed me in position to meet other guys from other cities and towns. Eventually, I could connect with them to broaden my drug organization. One of the things I realized while sitting in prison was that trouble traveled in packs. So, upon my release I made a conscious effort not to go back to hanging with the old crew as much as I did before. I mean we were still cool, but my role was a little different. I became more so a supplier and close associate. At this point, Reek and I became real close. While I was in prison him and my man Fox used to come visit me. They never failed to ask me when was I coming home. Since I was gone, they had no choice, but to go down to South Hoke and cop from them dudes from down there, but they really was not feeling it. As soon as I came home, I was served with some papers from the court saying I was being sued by a furniture company for failure to make payment. If I paid the amount by that coming Friday, I could avoid having to go before a judge. I was tired of looking these crooked judges in the face. So, I told Reek that we were going to pull all-nighter until I came up with $1,100 to pay for the furniture, and after that it was on and popping. By the end of the week, we had enough to pay off the furniture and enough left to by a slab. Honestly, it takes a real friend to invest all that have in their friends with only the hopes of making it to the top. Reek respected my hustle and knew how I moved so convincing him really wasn't that hard to do. Back then, we were taking trips back and forth to Greensboro every day to get one ounce of "crack" for $800. I had a little bit more clientele than he did which allowed me to get rid of mine a little faster than him. Which meant, I had to take a few more trips to Greensboro he did. Most of the time, he would ride with me, and put what he had with mine to cut down on the extra trips. Sometimes, we would even go twice in the same day depending on how fast we moved the work. As soon as I got $800 and enough money for gas, we were on highway 220. Depending on how late it was we would go get the dope, and sleep over at my man crib and hit the highway home the next morning. We did that for a while. I remember one time, there was a drought and we were going everywhere looking for some work. We went to Robeson County, Fayetteville, and Greensboro, but still couldn't find any. Then my cousin called and asked me if I had gotten straight yet, and I told him "no." So, he was like let me call my nephew in Laurinburg. So, he called him and he was like "yeah my people got some." So, Reek and I took the trip to Laurinburg, to go see what buddy was talking about. When we arrived, he jumped in the car and was like "it's just down the road." So, we started driving down 15-501, and I'm figuring we're going to Southern Pines or in that area. So, we get to Southern Pines and he was like "it's just a little bit down the road." Don't you know this dude tricked us into taking him to Durham. But when got there, he got up with his brother who had a music studio in the city.

Eventually, he became a celebrity DJ and was on shows like Rap City,106 and Park. He also had a cameo in Paid in Full and through his affiliation with Dame Dash, and was recently on the show Music Moguls with Dame Dash, Snoop Dog, Birdman and Jermaine Dupree. So, we meet up with his brother and eventually got straight. But the work was real thin and cut to death with baking soda. Because of the texture of the cocaine we gave them the name "Puddy Dud Boys." We only went to them as a last result. But during this process one of my partners turned me onto my man Big, from down in the country. This was an amazing opportunity because it was so close and I could make several trips on the same day without it taking up a whole lot of time. By this time, I was buying like four and a half ounces at a time. I was paying like $3500 for it so that was a pretty good price at the time. I was going down there like three or four times a week. At this point, I was pretty much locked in until something better came along. I had been all over the world buying drugs. I took a bus trip to Baltimore before, because there was a drought. I was like nineteen, when I took the bus to Baltimore. I didn't see one police the whole trip to Baltimore on the bus. When I got there, I bought seven ounces from some dude that my cousin turned me on to. On the way back in Richmond, I stepped into bus station and there were police everywhere with drug sniffing dogs and everything. What in the world was I going to do. I walked in the station and sat my bag down on one end of the station, and I went to the other end of the station. I walked outside of the station to plan me a little escape route just in case I had to run up out of there. I got on the phone and called a few people I knew just to calm my nerves. By this time, the police with the dog started walking through the terminal. When he got by my bag the dog walked past it, and turned back and smelled my bag. My heart was pounding, but he turned and kept walking. When they called out my bus number, I quickly grabbed my bag and hurried to get on my bus. I placed the bag at the front of the bus and sat in the back. I called Reek when we got to Dunn and told him to be at the bus station in Fayetteville. When we arrived in Fayetteville, Reek was nowhere to be found. I grabbed my bag and began walking. I felt like the faster I got out of that terminal the better. Reek finally picked me up, and when I walked up by the Market House. I've taken trips to DC, Baltimore, and New York, but Big was the most dependable, reliable and closet connect I've had up until that point. I mean after so many transactions we became really good friends. But "Big" was one of those guys that would hustle for a while stack his money then quit for a while. I mean could always fall back on gambling to maintain his lifestyle and relevancy in the game. But honestly, I can say it worked based on the fact that he never did any long sentences in prison like the rest of us that was getting money around that time. So, with "Big" out of the game, I was back looking for another connect which really wasn't that hard being that I was always networking. Plus, I had done really stacked my money up dealing with "Big". So, around the end of the 1998", I got plugged with this young Kat in Fayetteville, but he was originally from Fairmont. Fairmont is a pretty small town, but I always tell people that there is a lot of money in these small towns in North Carolina. The crazy thing about it was this dude was still in high school, but he was basically a middleman for his uncle who really had that work. I was buying anywhere from an half a key to twenty seven ounces a week from him from December of 1998, until about July of 1999. We were cool, but the cocaine was whack, I knew it was just a matter of time, I was going to get Buddy I just didn't know when. And I really didn't think it was going to come after my own misfortune. So, the first part of 1999, Reek and I were doing pretty good, money was coming in from left and right, and we had it all the clothes, jewelry, and plenty of women to me was a really exciting time. Around March of that same year, the boy Jay came back around talking about he had a connect in Texas getting keys for $18,000 a piece and he had been down there a couple of times already. He immediately caught my attention with the price being that I was paying as much as $28,000 for one already. My mind was already calculating. He was like "if you give me your money, I'll go down there and bring you one back". But I've been in the game long enough to know that he was getting them a whole lot cheaper than $18,000, but what it was is, he needed my money to get his for a much cheaper price and to convince the connect that he had more money than he actually had. But it was cool because I was already paying like $28,000 anyway. Around this time, I was worth around

$30,000 to $33,000. Not bad for a twenty- year old. So, he explained to me how they flew down to Texas, got the cocaine and flew back with it strapped it around their waist which would take roughly a week. Once I got the details I was all in. A few days later, he called and told me he was ready to make that move. I told him to meet me at the crib so, I could give him the bread. After a couple days he called me and told he was going to be a little longer than he expected. I ain't going to front, I was starting to get a little nervous. To make matters worse, I had people calling me from all over wanting some work. These dudes from Red Springs in particular was ringing my phone off the hook. I kept them on the hook, by telling them it would be in the morning. After about a week, Jay called and told me he had made it back. He sent my man "Big Head" over to get me and take me to his girlfriend's apartment over in the Ville. When we got there, he pulled the cocaine out of a duffel bag and handed it to me. My eyes lit up like a light bulb. I mean There it was right before my eyes "my first brick. For those that don't know, that was like a major milestone for anyone in the game, but for a twenty year old at time was almost unheard of. That had to be one of the greatest rides home ever! All I could think about was how I was going to get rid of that kilo real fast and send Jay down there, but this time I was going to get two keys. Man, that was going to be a lot of money. When I got home, I immediately took the kilo into my spare bedroom and busted the bag open. My aunt who was there with me could smell the chemicals in the cocaine all the way on the other end of the house. She came on my end of the house and said "boy I don't know what you got in there but that stuff is strong." So, now I had to find someone to cook it up for me. To be honest, I didn't know who in the area was capable of cooking up that much cocaine. I decided to give my man Parker a try. I got to Parker crib and as usual, it was flooded with crackheads and people coming in and out. When we got in the kitchen, he pulled out a little mason jar and placed it on the stove. My exact words to him was "we have too much cocaine to cook, to use that little jar, we'll be here all night." By this time, the boys from Red Springs called me again asking me if I was straight yet. I told him yeah, and asked him who was cooking his up. When he told me, I asked him to ask him if he would cook some for me too. He called me back and told me yeah. So, I told him to come get me because at time my car wouldn't crank. While I was waiting, I decided to ride my four wheeler to the store to get some bags and razor blades. When I got back, him and my other man was sitting in the yard. I got in the truck with them, and we rode down to Red Springs. When we got there my man Big Ken came and bought four and a half ounces of powder. In the meantime, we took a couple of grams and cooked it up just to see how good it was. After that my man from St. Paul's bought eighteen ounces. By this time, I had made about $17,700. It was a drought, so I could charge pretty much what I wanted to charge. By this time, another dude came in who I really wasn't familiar with, even though I had seen him at the racetrack a couple of times. It's crazy because now the dudes that I went down there for didn't even want to buy anything. My man from St. Paul's who I rode down there with asked me, if I was good and I told him yeah. At this point, I'm still not getting any bad vibes because we've done business before in the past and everything always went smooth. So, man told me he was locking up the house and for me to meet him out by the car. When I walked outside the dude that I knew from the track was standing by the door. He pulled out a black .38 and stuck it in my side. With a real aggressive tone, he told me to go back inside. When I got back inside the house he took the bag I had with all the money and the cocaine I had left in it. He made me lay down on the floor and put my hands behind my back. The whole time I was praying for him not to kill me, because to be honest, if it was me I probably would have killed me. He took the gold chain that I had around my neck and smashed my cell phone on the floor and stomped on it. By this time, he ran out of the house and jumped into his car. When I got to the door, he was speeding off around the corner. I immediately grabbed my phone to see if it was still working. While I was dialing Reek to tell him what happened, a crackhead came around the house trying to get the dude that was supposed to take get my car. I snatched the keys out of his hand and told him to get out of my face. So, I took the car and drove back to Raeford. When I got home, I called Reek and told him what happened. That night I got my aunt's car and rode back down there looking for them at all their little spots. Of course, I didn't find them but I was already thinking about my get back. Ol boy kept calling my phone talking about getting his car back which was a brand new 1998 Nissan Maxima. I was like "man you not getting your car until I get my money and my dope back." That went on for a couple of days until they started calling my house threatening my aunt to the point she was scared. Being that I knew I wasn't going to always be around to protect her, I decided to take the car back. I took the car and dropped it off at McDonald's in Red Springs and pissed all over the front seat. Little did they know my get back was already in motion. With the $12,000 or so that I had left I kept on buying drugs from the kid from Fairmont. Once I got my money back up to around $20,000, I called him and told him I needed twenty-seven ounces, but I lied and said that half of them was for my man in Laurinburg. He told me to meet him at Phat Daddy's in Fayetteville around seven o'clock. So, I went to the bank and got three- hundred dollars, worth of one- dollar bills. I took the money home and put nineteen one- dollar bills in a stack and put a twenty dollar bill on top and wrapped a rubber band around it until all the ones were gone. I put the money in a plastic bag and headed towards Phat Daddy's. On my way there, a dude I was locked up with called me and told me he had just came home from prison. I immediately took the detour and went and picked him up. I was thinking that was perfect timing. I could use him for reinforcements and he wouldn't even know it. When we got there ol boy pulled up a few minutes later. He threw the bag with the drugs in it in my car and I threw the bag with the money in it into his car and we drove off in different directions. Only thing is the money bag was about $20,000 short. I gave my man that rode with me a gram and dropped him back off at home. Before I could get home ol boy called me and was like "man what's going on" I immediately started riffing. When I finished he was like "for real Pistol man?" "I thought maybe it was your man from Laurinburg that put the okie doke in the game." Then I went home and poured out all the drugs onto my bed and just lavished in what I had just done. I mean I was from Robin Heights and we were down for whatever. But my victory party didn't last long. As I was sitting there gloating something said "look out the window." When I looked out the window I saw oh boy's car ride by my house. I'm thinking like how this dude know where I live. Later I found out he went to McDonald's in Raeford and asked some girls where I lived and they gave him the directions. So, I grabbed my gun and the drugs and ran out of the back door into the woods behind my house. By this time, he came back and pulled his car beside the road. When he got out I saw him tuck his gun in his waistline. I called my aunt who was inside the house that if anyone came looking for me to tell them I wasn't home. While I was still on the phone I could hear him knock and ask if I was home. After my aunt told him I wasn't, he got back into his car and left. I ran into him later that year on Christmas Eve in the mall. Reek and I was coming out of Foot Locker with about four or five bags in each hand when I turned he was headed right towards me. I immediately turned and told Reek he was coming. He asked me what was I going to do. I told him to come on. I turned and walked straight up to him and asked him what was up. He said I see you doing good." I was like "ain't, I'm supposed to be doing good." He asked me when was going to give him his money and I told him I already told him he wasn't getting any money. He showed me the gun he had in his waistline and was like " man if it wasn't for these police in here I would kill you right now." I told him to bad and walked off. When we got to the door we took off running to the car. I saw him one other time after that but that was it. I heard he got picked up by the Feds a short time after. With the money from that lick, I ended up paying cash for a white Acura Legend. For real for real that was my dream car. I used to tell my aunt that I wanted a white Acura Legend and she used to say that was a dope boy's car. At the time, I had started dating this chick that was a lot older than me even though almost all the women I date were much older than me. But before we started dating I was already in the process of moving to Greensboro. So really the whole time we dated I was back forward from Greensboro to Raeford. I would come home and buy my drugs and put them in my stash spot. Around this time, I was basically moving all drugs through Reek. He would just go get what he needed and whenever I came home he would have the money for it. Then I called myself quitting the game, but trying to take care of two houses was causing a real strain on the money I had saved. Then I lost a whole lot of money on one of them Texas runs. This older Kat around the way was running drugs out of Texas and he came to me to put in with him to buy a couple keys for the low. But on the way back the truck ended up getting stopped and the police found the pounds of weed that was on the truck, but not the cocaine. He ended up sending someone down there to burn the truck up before the authorities found it. That was a devastating blow. I ended up trying to sell my Acura to get some money to re-up. Luckily, I ended up going to prison for a possession of a firearm charge that I had caught earlier that year. So, in January of 2000, I went to prison for a year in custody of North Carolina Department of Corrections. While in prison I was hustling like I was still on the streets. I mean I was selling weed, cigarettes, and I owned all the card games on the yard. Then I messed around and got work release and was really able to save some money. I was making a enough money while in prison hustling to still send home. Reek and myself were both doing time, but I came home about a month before he did. Two weeks after I came home, I sat in my car and witnessed the police bust my mother for possible drug activity. Minutes before they raided, we got into a argument about her selling drugs. I told her she didn't need to be doing that because she had kids. I told her if I went to jail, I was going by myself but if she went my two sisters were going with her. My point was her going to jail was going to affect more than just her. Her last words to me was " you do you the way you do you, and let me do me the way I do me." I left out of the backdoor crying. Two weeks later, she got busted again. Both times, I had to put up money that I really didn't have in order to bail her out. Again, I was starting over already in the hole. At first my man "Big" fronted me about a ounce and a half, but he was on me so bad about his money that I knew I wasn't doing that again. I made a couple trips to Greensboro and bought so work from up there. When Reek came home trips became more and more frequent. During this time dudes were doing a lot of whooping. That's when dudes really cook the crack with little water and a lot of baking soda to stretch it to more than it actually was. Some people refer to it as dry cooking. Everybody and I mean everybody was whipping. We were taking frequent trips to Greensboro buying ounces for $800 a piece. Some may consider that extreme, but it made since to us because ounces were going for $1000 around the way. I mean the $200 minus the money for gas we were saving for making those trips would eventually add up. Think about it, after four trips we were roughly saving enough money to buy another ounce. We eventually hooked back up with my man Big and he turned us on to Mexican Johnny. Big used to always say "the Mexicans act like ni$$as now. When they first started, they were cheap now they wanna charge the same price as ni$$as." We were paying like $24,000 per kilo which wasn't bad, but there were dudes selling bricks for a thousand or two more. We used to get up early in the morning and go holla at the Migos. Now, the Mexicans used to hustle out of these ran down apartments back up in the cut between Lumberton and Rex Rennert. I remember one morning specifically, we were going there, and when we got there the FEDS were everywhere. I immediately placed the car in reverse and backed out there as fast as I could. We ended up going back a couple of days later, and got the story of how the Feds came and arrested Mexican Johnny and a few other Migos. It was so crazy, because back then you could be in there buying a kilo, and the guy beside you could be buying on rock. My man used to say that the migos were straight "Hot Boys." One of the biggest issues we had back then was, we couldn't cook so, we were always struggling to get someone to cook for us. That's why a lot of times, we always bought it already cooked up. That changed when we started dealing with the migos. I remember one time, we got some work and had my Burg from the Ville come and cook it up for us. Now Burg was a master chef, I mean whip master. We would take nine ounces and whip it back to twelve sometimes thirteen. With three/four extra ounces it wasn't that hard to get your weight up. This particular time, he couldn't get the work to locked up. We were at my uncles house over in Clay-hill so, I took 9 ounces out of the pot and took it back to the migos, and told him it wasn't right. He ended up giving me another kilo. He asked me did I want the pot back, I told him he could keep it. In my mind, I was thinking "I just got nine free ounces I can go buy me another pot." In the process of all this happening, Big had introduced me to the boy "Dough" from down in the country. I mean, we hit it off from the beginning. After that incident happened with the migos, I just started buying work from Dough and paying him $1000 cook them up for me. You probably think that's a lot, but when you consider the fact that everyone he cooked was coming back, at least four and a half ounces over a thousand dollars was nothing. One time I had one brick to come back nearly nine ounces over. The migos, he was dealing with used to get their keys from Texas. They would drive several trucks down there and bring the cocaine back inside the truck battery. They would crank the truck up, and take the real battery out and put the battery with the drugs in there and drive back. The only problem is they couldn't turn the truck off until they reached their destination. For that reason, when we called, we would ask if he had that battery. That was our code word to let him know we needed to get straight. I eventually got to the point where I was buying two to three keys at a time from him. This was around the time, I went and bought the Escalade. The dudes in the hood used to try and figure out how much money I was worth. They used to make bets that they could tell how much I was worth. One time, they told me they knew I was working with a brick. I told them they would know when I was working with brick, because I would have that Cadillac Escalade. So, when I got the Escalade they thought I was working with a brick, but I was actually working with two. You never let them know exactly what you're was working with. You gotta keep them guessing. When I first got the Escalade, I rode through the hood and stopped at my cousin's house. My uncle walked up to me and asked me what have I went and done. I was like "what you talking about." He said "don't you know them white folks downtown don't have one of these?" He said "man there is nowhere you can go where people are not going to want to know who you are." My response to him was "that's why I bought it."

Close Call:

It was the fall of 2002, Reek had just bought a red Acura Legend from this girl around the way. We were in that place where were dealing with the migos in Rennert, but it was hard finding someone to cook up our drugs. I mean there were cooks in the area, but not that many that could cook up that much at one time. I called my man from Red Springs and told him to find my man Bo and tell him I needed him. With that being said he told me to meet him in Thunder Valley trailer park right outside of Red Springs. So, Reek decided to drive the Acura, even though it didn't have any insurance on it. What he did was take the tags off his truck, and put them on the car. When we got to Thunder lley, we pulled up to a single wife trailer right at the entrance of the trailer park. We sat in the car waiting for my man and Bo to get there. When they arrived, we all went inside to start cooking up the key. While we were at the stove cooking, I walked over to the sink and looked out of the window. When I looked out the window I saw a silver Durango park behind Reek's car. I turned around and told the fellas that the police were outside. Their response was " how do you know?" I told them "because it's a silver Durango in the yard." By this time, he began knocking at the front door. We all stood still and got real quiet. So, the police stood there banging at the door. It's crazy because we started scrambling around in the house trying to get all the dope together. I took the dope we had already cooked and started stashing some of it in the vents in the floor and in the back of the toilet. All I could see was my picture on the front page of the newspaper with the headline "Drug dealer caught with a kilo of cocaine. By this time, the police was making his way around the house peeking in the windows. I was so scared that I knocked the broom down and it grabbed a whole of the curtain and left the window wide open allowing the police to look straight in the window. I stood against the wall beside the window on my tip toes trying to avoid being seen. My heart was pounding like a bass drum in the Turkey Parade. Next, he went around to the back door and began knocking. Bo then reached under his shirt and pulled out a gun and cocked it. I said "what you going to do with that?" He said "if he come in here, I'm going to shoot him." I said "not with me in here you ain't, man put that gun up." The officer kept going from the front door to the back down knocking and looking in the windows. Bo then requested that we run out of the back door and across this big field once he came back to the front door. I told him no because their was another police standing beside the trailer. He was like "how do you know, "I was like "I just know it." I crept to the back room and found Reek and my man from Red Springs hiding in the bed. I told them to get up so we could go. Bo said, "if we made it across the field we could go to a guy name Rabbit's house and hideout there". By this time, the police walked back to his truck and the other police walked from beside the trailer and got into the truck. They left and drove down the street and hid down in a ditch. I immediately started grabbing all the dope up and stuffing it in my book bag. We still had some dope in the pot on the stove. So, I took a towel and grabbed the pot off the stove. The police tried to fake like they were rushing to another call. I took the book bag and jumped out of the front door clearing every step with the pot with dope in still bubbling as I ran across the field to Rabbit's house. We went out into his garage and pretended like we were working on a car while the police kept riding by. We later called Nasha to come get us. I put the dope in the car with him and Reek and I caught a ride with someone else. I meet up with them at the county line once we were out of harms way and got into the car with them. When I got in the car, Nasha said "man you think you're slick, you gonna put all that dope in the car with us for us to get caught with it." I just laughed and said "man you crazy!"

Mexican Connect:

I dealt with Dough for about a year or so, before I got introduced to another migo that lived right in my hometown. A dude from my neighborhood was living beside the Mexican in a trailer park, and they became real cool with one another. My homeboy was getting weed from the migo, and a little coke every now and then. He eventually turned me and Reek on the migo. I started out buying a kilo from the Mexican just to try it out. We got in so good with the Mexican, and I started having him deliver it to my spot. We would still buy drugs from Dough from time to time depending on if the migos where straight or not. One night, I called the Mexicans around seven o'clock one night to bring me a couple keys, but he said he couldn't because the place was closed, and he didn't have access to them. In my mind immediately, thought to myself he must be keeping his cocaine inside one of those public storage buildings. I knew because it's been times when I thought about keeping mines there. I called Reek and told him where the migos kept their work, and we was going to get it. I immediately started putting my plan in motion. I called the migo and told him to bring me a brick to the spot. The whole time Reek was parked at the end of the street waiting on him to come by. The plan was to follow the migo and find out which storage facility, he kept the drugs in. I knew it was somewhere down 401, I just didn't know exactly which one.

Whenever we made a transaction with the migos, he would usually come and get the money and leave. A short time later, he would return with the cocaine. While Reek was waiting at the end of the street, I had Whoodie waiting at O'Berries to resume following him down 401. By this time, I would have had time to run and jump into my girlfriend's car that I had parked on the next block over. When he came and got the money, I immediately called Reek and let him know he was coming. Once he passed by Reek, his job was to follow him and call Whoodie just before they got to O'Berries so, he could already be on 401. Migo could just ride by him and he continue the chase and Reek could fall back. At this point, I would race down 401 and pick up the last end of the tail. Once I got into the car, I tried calling Reek to see how things were going, but I couldn't get no answer. I tried calling back still no answer. Then I tried calling Whoodie to see if he heard from Reek yet. His response was no, but they just rode by. So, I'm flying down 401 trying to catch up. The idea was to keep changing up who was following so, migo wouldn't think he was being followed. They made it all the way up by the Raeford Inn. But by this time, he realized he was being followed. See the car Reek was driving had those green fall lights on the front which made it easy for him to be noticed. So, what he did was make a sharp right turn and when he got into the curve he made a quick U turn and drove back past Reek going in the opposite direction. Man, I was furious! Reek and I ended up meeting each other at one of the stop signs near Puppy Creek fire department. I got out of the car in a rage. I asked Reek what happened and why his phone kept going to voicemail. His response was he was on the phone with some girl. That made me even more furious. We just missed the opportunity of a lifetime behind some chick. Before I could really express my disappointment, I realized I had to get back to meet the migo at the spot. When he came back I tried to play it off real cool, but I could tell he was a little suspicious.

The Sweetest Lick Ever!!

A couple months later, about two weeks from Christmas there was a drought. We were really at a stand- still. It was almost impossible to find any drugs. I was the type that was willing to travel anywhere I needed to go in order to get what I needed. One night, I was sitting at the crib when I got a phone call from Reek. He was telling me that a guy around the way called him, and said his brother just got back from Texas with a couple keys. When he told me who it was, I was like "man stop playing", but I used some other choice words. Reek insisted that we go check him out. After much convincing, I finally agreed to go. Now the reason why I was so hesitant, is because the guy was a crackhead and he had a peg leg. So, in my mind I thinking there is no way, this dude has any cocaine that he hasn't smoked yet. Let alone any keys. So, we took the trip over there. We got to the trailer park, we pulled up to this trailer about the size of two cars put together. So now I'm really thinking we're going on a wild goose chase. When we pulled into the yard, I noticed a old green Chevy Cavalier sitting on blocks with the hood missing and no motor. When I got inside ol' boy went and came back with a green army duffel bag and slammed in on the table. He opened the bag and began slamming kilo after kilo wrapped in grey duck- tape on the table, with 10 in total. My eyes got bigger than a Easter egg. He was like "there you go!" I said "how much you want for them?" He was like "get me $20,000 a piece." I was like "man I ain't giving you no $20,000." He said "how much you going to give me?" I said "$10,000." He was like "man they're worth more than 10,000." I said " that's all I got." In the meantime, he went and got a knife out of the dish rack and started sniffing the cocaine off of the knife like he was Scareface or somebody. But while I was looking at the kilos, I suddenly recognized something about them. The way they were wrapped looked real familiar. So, I had to try my hand. I looked him in the eyes and said I know who this work belong to. He was like "who?" I said "this migo dope and if migo find out you got his dope he going to kill you." I said " that's them California Mexicans and if they find out you got their dope they going to kill you." He said this ain't no migo dope, my brother just got back from Texas with this dope." I said "that's migo dope and know where you got it from." I said "you got it out of one of those public storage buildings." I said I know because I tried to get it." I said "I tell you what, I bet if you cut this one, this one, and this one open (pointing at three of them) I bet they got milos written on them." He was like "milos?" I was like "yeah milos, that's bad in Spanish." He said bad! ain't none of these bad. I told him, I bet when you cut the grey tape off it's wrapped inside a red balloon. When cut the tape off the first one it was wrapped in a red balloon. When he took it out of the balloon there it was milos. His eyes got bigger than a 50 cent piece. So, now I'm getting a little cocky. I pointed to another one and said "cut it open." When he cut it open the same thing "red balloon." When he took the balloon off it had milos written on it. And the same thing for the third. When he lifted up his head in amazement, I looked him dead in his eyes and said with my teeth clutched together "Migo, gonna kill you!" With fear in his voice he responded "how much you gonna give me for them?" I said "I told you $10,000." Now that I think about it, he was so scared I probably could have got them for a whole lot cheaper. I told him "I'll be back let me run to the crib and get the money." I immediately got on the phone and started making phone calls. The first person I called was Dough. I said "man what's good, you straight?" He was like "nah I'm still waiting." I said "boy I just ran across a sweet lick." He said "I need three what's the number?" I said $20,000." He said "bring them on." So, Reek dropped me off at the crib while he went to get his money, and I made arrangements to have my money brought to me. When Reek got back, we rode over there and dropped off $100,000 to Oh buddy! Before I left I told him not to go spending money like he was crazy, but to wait a couple of weeks and let things blow over a little bit, and he could do what he wanted. He said "man I gotcha" and me Reek left. We went out into the country and sold three to Dough for $60,00. We took the money and split it 30,000 a piece. Reek called me about nine o'clock the next morning, talking about he just went a bought a new Lexus; and I won't believe he who he just saw buying a Chevy Tahoe and was on his way to get some music put in it. I was like "who?" He was like "ol Boy we just got the dope from." I was like "for real?" "Man, I told that dummy not to go spending money like he was crazy." I got up and went by my mother's house and told her what happened. She took her time, and listened to me, but as soon as I finished explaining what happened she politely stuck her hand out and said "now give me some money." I laced her hands with a couple twenties and went and got in my truck. The next day my momma called me, and said Mike "ol Boy" tripping. I said "what you talking about?" She said she just got a phone call from one of my exes and she told her that she was at the store getting gas and ol Boy was in front of her buying gas. She said he gave the girl behind the counter a $100 for $20 worth of gas and told her to keep the change. When the girl asked him if he was sure, she said he opened a big bag of money and showed it to her and said, "yeah I'm sure." I was like this dude is going to get us killed! I wanted to see how damaged he had done, so I rode over to that little trailer he was living in. When I got there, I was amazed at what I saw. The Cavalier that was on bricks now had a set of 18 inch rims on it, and it still didn't have a hood or motor. Later that evening, I called the migo and told him to bring me a brick. I did that often for the next couple of weeks just play it off. I didn't want him assuming that it was me that had his dope. That next weekend, as soon as I walked in the club there he was standing there with a mink coat on and his arms around to women. When he saw me, he yelled out "what's up big money." I immediately turned around and walked out of the club. I didn't want to be seen talking with him. So, I left and went home. Two week later, he called me asking about $500 that I owned him. I told him to come get it. When he got there, he told me he had something for me. He walked to the back of his Tahoe and lifted up the back door. When he opened it, he had a truck full of fake Timberlands he had stole from some department store. I said man I can't do nothing with that. He kept begging me to take them off his hands. I lied and told him to come see me the next day. As he left, I stood there shaking my head. I couldn't believe it, this man was broke. A hundred thousand dollars gone just like that. That was a great Christmas. I had just took a major loss in Atlantic City during Thanksgiving. I went Christmas shopping for me, my girl and her two kids in New York. After that, we decided to take a trip to Atlantic City. While we were there the valet at the casino broke into my truck, and stole everything we bought plus he took one of the television out of my truck and damaged the rest. So, we had to go back and replace everything we bought and I had to get my tv's fixed. That was a little over $10,000 replacing all of that. Reek took his money and bought a Chevy Avalanche and threw some 24's on it. A couple of weeks later, I got a call from Venny who was the leader of the Mexican cartel in the area asking me, if I had seen or heard his nephew. I told him no and he asked me where I was, and if he could meet me somewhere to talk. I told him to come to the spot. When he got there, he asked me to take a ride with him. So, I got in the truck and we went for a ride down 401. While we were riding, he began telling me how his nephew took two keys and disappeared on him. He then told me I was right about the keys being about a ounce short. He said he didn't believe me at first, but then he started getting calls from other people saying the same thing. He said his nephew was taking a knife and shaving an ounce out of every key and selling them on the side. He said but that's not even the half. He said about two months ago, thirteen got missing out our stash spot, and he said he believes you had them. I was like "what!" He said yeah, he said one night he came to meet you, and when he left someone was following him but he lost them. But he said, but now I know it was that little prick and he was trying to put it on you. I just shook my head. We rode to the county line and turned around. On the way back, he said he had some other Mexicans that owed him some money, and they just got twenty keys in from Arizona. He proposed that if I helped him rob them, he would split them with me. I told him I would, but in the back of my mind I was thinking "man I'm letting you get me nowhere and kill me." When we got back to my spot, as I was getting out of the truck he said said "P" from now on, I'm only going to charge you $21,000 for each key. I said "that's what's up" and got out of the truck. A few hours later, I got a call from his nephew. I said man " your uncle is looking for you." He said "I know but yo! I'm straight now." "Any time you need something I got it." I was like "what's the number?" He said the same as before. With that in mind, I decided to play one against the other to negotiate a better price. So, I told him his uncle said I could get them for $21,500. So, he said he would do them for $21,000. So, when his uncle called me a few days later I told him I had another connect that was letting me get them for $21,000 so, he dropped the price to $20,500. When I called his nephew back he was like "come on "P" I can't go no lower than that. So, I was like "alright I'm going to get at you." We dealt with them from time to time. But after I got the club in Southern Pines, Reek went and bought a 18 wheeler. The guy he had driving for him had been driving for a long time, and had connections all over from dealing with other drug dealers in the past. He made a few phone calls and got in touch with one of his old connects. We ended up getting a connect in Texas getting kilos for $15,000 which was a whole lot lower than what we were getting them for in the area. With that type of price, I could sell kilos for anywhere from $23,500-$24,000 sometimes $25,000 depending on who it was, and make at least $8000 for each kilo I sold. I was buying anywhere from three to five kilos every week, which meant I was making anywhere from

$24,000 to 40,000 a week. I had a guy from Massey Hill in Fayetteville buying four kilos at a time, and another guy from the Murk buying at least one. I had another homeboy from Laurinburg buying a half kilo, but he wanted his already cooked up. I had a dude from Virginia buying nine ounces and another dude from Laurinburg buying nine ounces. Whenever the driver was gone to Texas, and somebody wanted something I would just go buy a kilo from the migos or Dough to make the quick sale. With all this going on, I started feeling like it was all coming to an end. It was times, I would get in my truck and ride out in the country by myself drinking a six pack of Coronas and just talk to God. I mean here I was with all this money, I had plenty of women, I could go anywhere I wanted to go, but it was still something missing. God, what is it. I mean I used to be in the club full of people, but I felt like I was the only one in there. What I was missing was God. He is the only thing that can bring fulfillment or satisfaction in your life.

The Jump Off:

In February of 2003, I decided to open up a night club. I figured since I went to the club three or four times a week, I could run a club. I got with my old head Gary, and spoke to him about what I had planned and that I wanted him to be my front man. He agreed, and we started putting the plan in motion. On February 14, 2003 The Jump Off opened. It was a fun time. We definitely had a lot of fun, and made a lot of money but not without its challenges. I had bartenders and the people at the door steal money from me. One time twenty cases of Coronas got missing out of the cooler. I know they were there, because I put them there. But when I went to fill up the cooler they were gone. At the time, I was living in Greensboro, but I would come home on the weekends to open the club. One day my roommate, and I was driving from Greensboro to Charlotte, when I got a call from Reek saying that I needed to call Gary. I first thought was that the police had run down on him but Reek said "nah somebody broke into the club and stole the rent money." I was like "What?" " Man, ain't nobody broke into no club and stole no rent money. That club is like Fort Knox, you can barely get in there with a key." I called him and he tried to explain what happened which I wasn't trying to hear it. So, I told him I would be down there later. When I got there, I had Reek to come meet me to take me to meet him. When we pulled up beside him, I told him to tell me again what happened. He began to explain to me again what happened. When he finished, I looked at him and asked him if I was suppose to believe somebody broke in the club, and stole the rent money. I told him I'm going to tell you what happened. " You had one of those young girls in there and she put you to sleep, and took the rent money. He dropped his head and started nodding yes with tears coming down his face crying for me not to kill him. I said, " I'm not going to kill you, but you are going to pay me my money back." As we drove off, Reek rolled the window up and said, " why you got that grown man out here crying" we both started laughing, and drove off. The biggest challenge came one night, when some guys from Sanford was beating this boy from Southern Pines so bad; that I had to shoot up in the ceiling two times to keep them from beating him to death. I saved his life, but I killed the club. After that people were afraid to come out, so I ended up closing the club down.

God's Calling:

One day, I happened to be at the store when a lady pulled up and asked me to go in the store for her to get a can Pepsi because she was in a rush. She gave me fifty- two cents, but the soda was only fifty -one cents. So, I left out of the store with the Pepsi and the penny that was left over. I handed her the soda, and told her I was keeping the change. Then I said "nah!! here you go I'm good, I don't need it." And she was like "yeah everybody know you don't need no money." Then she said, "everybody know you're the man around here." Then I said, "I'm not the man." Then she said " yes you are, these boys will do anything you tell them to do." Then I was like " no they won't." She went on to say," I bet you if you called that boy over there and tell him to come here, he'll come, call him." So, I was like "Black come here!" When he came she said "told you." When he came, he started talking real disrespectful to her so, I told him to leave. When he left the lady started telling me how she had been meaning to stop by my house and talk to me. She said, "the Lord had been dealing with her about me". She said "God called me to preach His Word." I was like "I'm not doing no preaching." Then I was like "you know what if the church pay me seventy thousand dollars a year and buy me a 745, I'll preach." She was like ok, God heard that. She was like "God is about to sit you down." So, we started talking about God and the Bible. I asked her some pretty tough questions that she couldn't really answer. I didn't know what I was talking about, but I had done been in prison all that time with "Five Percenters and Muslims, so I used to listen in on their conversations. Some even went to the point of trying to convert me, so I had plenty of questions to try to discredit God and the Bible. As the conversation went on, another lady from the neighborhood pulled up and joined in the conversation. But the lady was talking about me hanging out at the store, smoking weed, and selling drugs. I told her that I've never smoked weed before and she's never saw me sell any drugs before. Her response was "I see you bent over into people cars all the time. So, I walked over and bent over into her car and I said "now I'm bent over into your car, but am I selling you any drugs?" You should have seen the look on her face. And when she pulled off the other lady said, "you got her that time." Then she said, "I got to get out of here I'm late, but remember what I told you."

† 2 WEEKS LATER †

I remember waking up a particular morning, telling Reek I would meet him later over Norm's house. Norm was my man that had a mechanic shop at the back of his house. The only problem is that once we started hanging over there no cars were being worked on. It's crazy because people used to come by checking on their cars, and they would still be parked in the exact same spot they were in the last time they came by. I mean we put a pool table inside the garage and turned it into a little juke joint. I got to Norm's house before Reek got there, because Norm was supposed to tinting the windows on my car that I got from the auction. It was a little Geo Prism, I had bought to ride around town in, because I didn't have driver's license. The thing is I never parked this car at my house, because I didn't want anyone to know I had this car. If they knew then the cops would know. While we were there, I pulled out my motorcycle and started doing burnouts in the middle of the street. By this time, Reek ended up coming and before long, he left on his motorcycle to go see his daughter, and it began raining. When he returned, he got in his car and left to go see his daughter. Hours after he left, I decided to go home and eat because my girl called and said she was finish cooking. Instead of driving my Lexus back home, I decided to drive the Prism. On the way home, I was going to park the car around the next street over at my aunt's house. When I got the something said, "just go ahead and drive the car home since you're not going to be there that long anyway." When I drove around the corner, I saw a silver unmarked car parked at the stop sign watching my house. I pulled up to the stop sign, came to a complete stop, put my turn signal on and drove off. I drove up the street and parked the Prism in my grandmother's yard, and walked home. When I got in the yard, I jumped in my Escalade and drove it around the house to keep the license plate from being seen from the street. When I came around the house and stopped, the unmarked car jumped out of his hiding spot to get behind me only to realize my truck wasn't moving, but the rims were still spinning. To play it off, he turned his blue lights on a sped away in the other direction as if he was going after someone. So, I ran out into the street to see which way he was going. He drove down the street and turned around and came back and parked in the same spot as before. So, I went through the back door and watched the unmarked car through the kitchen window as ate the bake fish and salad my girl had made for dinner. When I finished, I decided to go out the back door and walk through my mother in law's yard and come out at the store. While I was walking across my yard, Reek's sister in law pulled into my back yard in a panic and told me that the Feds got Reek! I told her that the car parked at the stop sign was them. When she backed out of the yard, the unmark car pulled he over supposing that I got into the car. I immediately ran through the woods behind my house, and came out at the store. I went to my cousin's house down the street. I wanted to get them to take me back to Norm's house to get my thoughts together. While there so many thought racing through my mind. I noticed that Reek left his other phone on top of his car. When I grabbed it, and it started ringing with people asking what happened. Of course, I lied and told them that he was in the hospital. Finally, I got in touch with his girlfriend, and she gave me the run- down of what happened. Apparently, when he got to his baby momma's house the Feds were already waiting on him. They waited until he got inside and busted in and arrested him. By this time, I got a call from my man from Massey Hill wanting four kilos. I told him it would be later on. My plan was to go to the library get four books, and wrap them in duck-tape and sell them to him. With that money and what money, I had left I could go on the run. I would just go to my apartment in

Greensboro, and hang out there for a couple of days. Then head to my girl's crib in Charlotte. With so many people in my ear, and not knowing who was who and what was what. I had my man to take me to Southern Pines to a girl's house, that I had been dealing with. My next move was to try to get rid of any incriminating papers or phone calls. I started taking receipts and other papers out of my pocket and burning them. Then I started erasing numbers out of my phone. She was a little familiar with the Feds because her ex-boyfriend was in federal prison. The only problem was, is that she had to go to work at eleven o'clock. So, I had Whoodi, and my cousin to bring me the Geo Prism and about $5,000 so, I could hide out for a while. After they left, I drove up to Biscoe to this other girl's house and spent the night there. That whole night the Raeford police kept running into my house looking for me. Every time someone would turn a light on, they would run in there thinking it was me. Things still didn't make since. I mean why would the Fed run down on Reek and not run down on me at the same time and give me a chance to run? Usually when the Feds make a bust, they run down on everyone involved at the same time. I later found out the reason was the Feds didn't have a warrant for me at the time. They were just watching to see what my next move was going to be. The next morning, I got up and drove to Greensboro and got in touch with a few lawyers and explained the situation. One lawyer said nine times out of ten, if the Feds have a warrant for your friend then they got one for you too. Man, that's the last thing I wanted to hear, I called Gerald Beaver and he said for me to give a few minutes to make a few phone calls, and he'll call me back. After about an hour or so, Mr. Beaver called me back and said that the Feds didn't have a warrant for me, but the state had one. He said that he spoke with the sheriff and he assured him that if I turned myself in, he would give me a bond. I asked Beaver how trustworthy was that? He said, he and the sheriff were good friends, and if he lied to him he would never speak to him again. So, I asked him what did he think I should do? He said "Micheal turn yourself in." So, I made my way from Greensboro to turn myself in. I made a stop at my cousin's job in Southern Pines to return the money, I had gotten from her. When I got out of the car people were looking at me real funny. Apparently, they had me on the news as an outstanding fugitive who was armed and dangerous. So, I left the Pines and went to the barbershop shop to get my haircut because I'm thinking I'm going to go down here, and get a bound and be out in time to go to the club that night. After I got my haircut, I called the sheriff and told him to come and get me from the barbershop. I also called my mother and told her where I was. So, while I'm waiting for the sheriff my mom pulled up riding with one of my exes. With the sheriff taking so long to come get me, I told my mom and my ex to drop me off at sheriff station so, I could turn myself in. My mother couldn't believe what I said. The whole time we were riding she kept saying "I just can't believe this." She said, "she would have never thought I would turn myself in". By the time we got there, and the sheriff and his deputy was coming out of his office. I said man y'all were taking too long. When the deputy grabbed me to put the cuffs on me, the sheriff waved his hand and said it was no need for that. He said, "Micheal Monroe you are under arrest for conspiracy to sell and deliver crack cocaine" and he read me my rights. Once inside we went into his office. He walked around and sat down at his desk made of shiny dark brown mahogany wood. He politely asked me to have a seat in one of two chairs sitting in front of his desk. While his deputy stood at the door behind me. When I sat down he asked me "what did I have to tell him. My response was "what you mean?" He said "you know, what information you got for me?" I said "man you already know I'm not telling you nothing." He said "I knew you were going to say that, that's why I called the magistrate and told him to shoot for the stars." Then he told his deputy to get me out of his office. It was there, that I realized I made a big mistake by turning myself in. When I got to the magistrate's office, I sat there in a chair with my hands handcuffed behind waiting for the magistrate to tell me my bond so, I can begin making arrangements to get out of there. As I sat there patiently waiting, the magistrate finally called my name and began quoting all these legal terms that I really wasn't concerned about. I do remember him saying that I wasn't a flight risk being that I've never missed a court date, and I don't own any visas or passports. But he said that "I was a threat to the community". And for that reason, this is your bond and he spun the paper around so I could see it. I leaned forward to take a quick glance at what the bond was. So in my mind I said "Oh, $100,000, I'll be out in no time." Something said "you better count those zeros again." So, I leaned forward again and began to count each individual zero nodding my head as I did it." Then I yelled out of nowhere, voice all high pitched "a million dollars?" "Man, I didn't kill nobody." From there they took me to the jail and placed inside the holding cell. So here I am sitting in jail under a million - dollar bond. At first, I was tempted to make the bond a go home which would have cost me about $150,000 cash money. But after talking to my lawyer, he advised me that that wouldn't be a smart move. He said if The Feds didn't have me, if I made that bond they were definitely coming to get me on if not anything else, tax evasion charges. After a couple hours of sitting there, they finally took me to my cell which was one of the old juvenile cells. As a matter of fact, it was the same cell that I was in the first time I ever went to jail. In jail they to never write your name on the walls because if you do you'll come back to see it again. In my mind, I'm thinking the saying is true. The cell was all dark and cold and the ceiling leaked when it rained. I called my lawyer and told him about these unsafe conditions they had me sleeping in, and he said he would get on it. During my first court appearance and bond reduction hearing the judge on duty stated that he couldn't deal with my bond reduction, because he was part of the reason it was that way. He said, "the sheriff called him and asked him to call the magistrate on duty and request a high bond in my case and he did. So, he was going to have to continue my bond hearing for another date, so another judge could handle it. They took me back to the jail, but after my lawyer spoke to the captain over the jail they put me in regular population. The whole Robin Heights was in there. But that didn't last long because with me being in there with other inmates, it was hard for them to monitor my phone calls. So, they eventually took me out of general population and put me in a isolation cell, so they could easily monitor my phone calls. At my next court appearance, things got a little exciting. First of all, the DA and the detectives took all day coming out because they were in there corroborating their story. We they finally came out, they had all these wild stories about the sheriff receiving all these threatening phone calls and one particular call from a hit man stated that I paid him $250,000 to kill the sheriff and the informant on my case. He also stated that the informants mother had been receiving threatening phone calls and unknown individuals have been coming to her house trying to get in. He stated, that I wrote a letter instructing my family to pay out large sums of money to my lawyer and my codependent's lawyer. My lawyer objected and said "your honor I can't dance with shadows." The judge sustained and asked the DA if there was any evidence of these accusations. The DA stated no there was no evidence. The judge said, "he was going to have to grant my bond reduction, but not to the $75,000 that my lawyer requested, but he was going to drop it to $500,000 because he said had to take the threat on the sheriff allegations into consideration". He said, he didn't want to release me and have something happened to the sheriff. But he said that the DA needed to have proof of those allegations by my next court date, or he was going to have to reduce my bond to the $75,000 requested by my attorney. Before my next court date, I was federally indicted and taken to a federal holding facility. That's where the infamous picture of me holding up my middle fingers came from. But while I was in jail, one of sergeants that I became very familiar with gave me a book to read called "The Divine Revelation of Hell. That book literally scared me to death. Then there was this officer that just started working in the jail. He used to come by cell every evening, and talk about the Lord and the Bible. He used to wear these Durango boots that used to make a distinct sound whenever he would walk down the hallway. Whenever I would hear him coming, I would grab my Bible off the floor, and pretend like I was reading it just to impress him. Whenever he would walk past my cell, and see me reading he would say "ok I see you." I was also memorizing scriptures to impress my family whenever I spoke with them on the phone. As if I was convincing them that I changed. I tell people all the time "I tricked myself into getting saved."

The Transformation:

I was escorted by the US marshals from the Hoke County jail. Shackled and handcuffed, I was placed in the back of a van much similar to a dog kennel with one other inmate. From there, we made a stop at McCain prison to pick up another inmate. An hour and a half later, we stopped at the jail in Ashboro, and picked up another inmate on our way to the federal holding facility. Once we got to the Guilford County jail in High Point, we we're taken out of the back of the van and placed in a holding cell until officers came and processed us in. I'll never forget it. I had on some blue jean shorts, all white Huaraches and a white and burgundy Bill Walton throwback jersey. The same clothes, I had on nearly two months ago when I was first arrested. The only difference is that now they were all wrinkled from sitting in a bag for so long. Once we were processed, we were taken to the fourth floor of this massive structure. I was placed in a two- man cell with two other inmates. I was the new guy so I was given the floor to sleep on. As I sat there, I became acquainted with my new cell mates. One night, as we were talking about God, and the Bible something just got a hold of me. I mean, I started crying and confessing all these things to God that I had done, and how I had treated people. When that moment was over, I felt like a weight had been lifted off of my shoulders. I felt like a new person. The jail I was in, was a twenty- one and three meaning, we were locked down in our cells twenty- one hours in the day, and out for three. I couldn't wait to get out the next morning to call my family and tell them I had gotten saved. It was the greatest feeling ever. From that day forward, I was just hungry for the Word of God. Anytime I would hear someone talking about the Bible I would stop and listen. My cell and I continued to read and discuss the Bible, and occasionally a officer would stop by and chop it up with us. From there, I was taken to the county jail in Winston Salem where a lot of my early growth came from. We were allowed to go to a structured Bible study three times a day. There were Pastors and Ministers from different churches brought in to teach Bible study. My favorites had to be Pastor "Rip," and the guys from St. Peter. We had a lot more freedom, which gave us an opportunity to sit down and have Bible study among ourselves. We had different guys there that had a pretty good understanding of the Bible, but none like Danny Lewis. This guy knew the Bible like the back of his hand. He could quote scriptures like crazy, and if you wanted to know where a scripture was, he could take you straight to it. I remember praying one night and saying "Lord I want to know the Bible the way Danny knows it and even better. From that moment on, it seems I could just memorize scripture without having to put forth any real effort. When I got to prison, I knew the Bible so well, they used to call me "Scriptures" and "The Walking Concordance".

On one occasion, one of the volunteers was a retired police chief from Greensboro. After hearing his testimony on how he got saved. The Holy Spirit spoke to me and said that I needed to contact him. I said "Lord if you want me to speak to this guy, you're gonna have to make a way for me to speak with him." The next day, I got called by the nurse into the room where we have Bible study and there laying on the floor was a business card. When I picked it up the card had the guy's name on it. And on the back it had "Call Me" written on it. Man, you wouldn't believe how excited I got. I never did get a chance to talk to him, but God was just showing me how good He was and everything would be alright if I would just trust him. After about four months, I ended up leaving Winston Salem and going to Guilford County jail in Greensboro. Now the jail in Greensboro was ridiculous. I mean, it was dirty and overcrowded. You probably had thirty people in an eight - man cell block. I mean you basically had to find a spot to lay your mat down to sleep. There were people sleeping on top of the table, under the table and on the two benches. There were also people sleeping from wall to wall, and everywhere in between. But because I was Winston Salem so long around such great teaching. I became the primary Bible study teacher in Greensboro. I mean the guys were amazed at how well I knew the Bible. I was thinking if you think I'm something you should have met some of those guys back in Winston.

Edgefield, South Carolina:

Eleven months later after a long drawn out process, I stepped onto a federal institution with a 216 month prison sentence and that's where the real journey began!! When I got to FCI Edgefield, the moment I walked through the gate it was like walking in the courtyard of a castle. All you saw was concrete walls and chain link fences. I was escorted to A building and assigned to my cell. I was placed in a cell with a young black guy from Miami. My other cell mate was a white guy that just finished doing twenty something years on state, and had to do five years in the Feds to complete his sentence. The only problem was that while, he was on state he got into a confrontation with a black guy because the guy was trying to turn him out. They ended up getting into a physical altercation and the white guy got the best of the black guy. Long story short, the deal was to squash the beef, but the black guy reneged and stabbed the white guy twenty times and hitting a main nerve which caused the white guy to just continuously shake. When my cell mate from Miami saw him walk through the door, he immediately went to the counselor and had his cell changed. On his way out, he urged me to leave as well. But being the good Christian guy that I was, I decided to stick it out. It was times when he would find myself cleaning up after he used the bathroom all over the toilet and floor. The guy from Miami used to say I was crazy. But I was doing my Christian duty. Then one night, I was up around ten o'clock reading my bible with the light on because that's what I did. Then, started complaining about the light being on. So, we started going back and forth about the light, stood up and turned the light off. I slowly got down off of the top bunk and turned the light back on. So, here I am going back and forth with this guy about a light. After I have been cleaning up behind him for about two weeks. I climbed back onto my bunk, he took it upon himself to start hitting me. At this time, I got down from off my bunk and hit the distress button. When the officer came I explained to him what had happened. Mike really couldn't talk because when he got stabbed the guy hit him in the neck causing him to mumble when he talked. We were taken to out of our cell, and to the Lieutenants office and placed in the "special housing unit" pending investigation. The next morning, a investigator came and questioned me about the incident and took pictures of the scratches on my arms and legs. After thirty days, I was cleared of any wrongdoing. I meet a lot of good brothers in Edgefied, one in particular we called twin. Twin was a tiny little fella, but he knew his Word and loved the Lord. He is the one that got me into using Bible dictionaries and concordances to study the Bible and look up words. I was only at Edgefield for six months, when they started taking requests to be transferred to FCI Bennettsville in Bennettsville South Carolina.

Bennettsville, South Carolina:

Bennettsville was only forty- five minutes from home so I put in my request to be transferred. My request was approved and on January 6, 2005, I was transferred to Bennettsville South Carolina along with thirty- four other inmates. For about two and a half months, we were the only ones on the entire compound which means we had first choice at all the great jobs. I got a job in the chapel because I wanted to work along -side, the chaplain and learn as much as I could. Now, the chaplain was this short little Puerto Rican guy who spoke broken English and wore a hearing aid. To make matters worse, he was slew-footed and often fell when he walked. Like what am I supposed to learn from this guy. But then there was brother Thompson. Brother Thompson and I became really close throughout the years, and I learned a lot from him. He was a master at taking bible stories and pulling lessons out them and making them relevant to any situation you might have found yourself in. But as time went on, other guys started coming to the prison, and before long there was sixteen hundred inmates running around on the yard. We were the first ones there, we had gained the chaplains trust and Thompson and myself had the responsibility of being like the inmate Pastors. Around April of that year, another brother came by the name of Lester. Now Lester, was and is one of the most laid back individuals you're ever going to meet. But he had so much power in voice. He had one of those real preacher voices. You know, the ones that sound like they got a bass drum down their throat. Lester came from FCI Talladega in Alabama, where he was the inmate Pastor there, so he fit right in with Thompson and myself. Later in the year, I was in the chapel sweeping the the foyer when this guy walked in wearing a prison uniform and a prison issued hat. He introduced himself as brother Dave, and asked if there were any Christian brothers there. I shook his hand and introduced myself. He immediately began talking to me about the Bible and asking me various questions. By this time, Lester walked by and I introduced him to the new brother along with brother Thompson. Him and Lester hit it off really well, and began spending a lot of time together. Thompson and brother Dave didn't really see eye to eye on a lot of things when it came to the Bible, and the how the church should be managed. I found myself in the middle of many theological debates ranging from once saved always saved to speaking in tongues. It was usually Thompson and myself versus Brother Dave and Brother Lester. We used to go out on the yard and have some slap down drag outs. It got so bad one time, that people were looking like listen to those Christian brothers over there. The more we debated the more I was learning. When I looked back, I could see how God was using these situations to teach me. As time went on, Brother Dave later became known as Apostle Fabian and I started attending his Bible studies on the yard from time to time. He started a Bible study on the yard because the chaplain wouldn't allow him to do anything inside the chapel. I watched as his Bible study grew from just him and Brother Lester to as many as fifteen to twenty people. He really believed in the power of God and began doing deliverance ministry and people were being set free from demonic spirits. I was very zealous for the things of God and wanted to see the people of God blessed and experiencing the abundant life that Jesus spoke about. One night, I was praying and I asked God why didn't we see the things happening today like we read about in the Bible. He said "they are, you just not where they're happening at." I asked the Lord where and he said "out there on the rec. yard." I immediately went and apologized to Apostle Fabian and submitted myself under his ministry. He immediately started teaching me everything he knew and giving me certain books to read. My spiritual life took off like a rocket. Of course, Thompson didn't like it and our friendship was a little strained. But at the end of the day, I had to do what was best for me. Thompson had taken me as far as he could take me, but now it was time for me to learn the ways of the Lord more perfectly. Apostle Fabian started training me and Lester in deliverance, and how to lay hands to heal the sick and impart the baptism of the Holy Ghost with the evidence of speaking in other tongues. We learned so much under Apostle Fabian's ministry in very short period of time. We learned about the five-fold ministry, spiritual gifts and the foundational doctrines for Christian living. We were trained in the prophetic and interpretation of tongues. This man was really before his time. After about a year in Bennettsville. Apostle Fabian was shipped to another compound. Thompson eventually left leaving Lester, and myself as the primary leaders over the Christian organization. By this time, brother Lane came and joined the fold along side me, and Brother Lester. We were like the three amigos. Lane was very protective over the church. He was letting nobody in who wasn't what they say they were. In 2009 or 2010, we meet another young brother named Antonio and he became the fourth amigo. We gave him the name "Little Scrappy" because he was always ready for a good Bible debate. It was a pleasure watching him grow into a prominent preacher and devout man of God. Man, we saw plenty of characters come and go throughout my bid. We had this one particular guy named Rouse who was a part of the praise team. It seemed like every time he got the mic to sing, the presence of God would just leave the room. For this reason, I gave him the name ikki short for Ichabod meaning the glory has departed. We also started teaching Bible study on the yard and doing deliverance ministry. We spent countless hours counseling guys after they lost love ones or their wives left them. They were more comfortable talking to us than they were the chaplains. But before we knew it another chaplain came who believed pretty much the way we believed, so everything was moved inside the chapel. It was at this time that we started getting opportunities to preach on Sunday mornings, and really exercise our gifts on a larger crowd. Apostle Fabian taught us how to study the Bible, and basically how to feed ourselves. He basically gave us our own curriculum to guarantee our spiritual growth and development. I woke up at 4:30 every morning, and prayed for a hour. Our cell doors were opened at 5:30. I started every morning out reading Psalms and Proverbs. From 7:00 to 7:50 I studied one book and then I took a ten minute break. Then from 8:00 to 8:50 another. I did this from 2006 until my release in 2013. Throughout my journey, I saw God move mightily in several people's lives. Even in my own life. I've seen God do some amazing things. One of the things God taught me while in prison is that, I didn't have to fight my own battle. There were several occasions where people wronged me and God revenged me. Prison taught me how to be content in any state that I found myself in. My life had changed so much that people used to ask me what I was doing in prison. I used say "what you think I'm in prison for selling bibles." I remember going to great lengths to convince people that, I was a different person on the street. Until the Holy Spirit spoke to me and said "why are you trying to convince them of who you used to be. The fact that they can't see is a testimony that you have changed." From that day forward, I stopped trying to convince people that my life had truly been changed. Christ that was born in me; had been formed in me. My life had truly been TRANSFORMED!!!

Afterword:

I believe, I had a pretty tight operation. All my drugs were stashed at secure location at my uncle's house. My money was stashed at my cousin's house, so if the police rushed the crib they wouldn't find anything. At this point, I stopped selling anything less than four and a half ounces and I stop dealing with people in Raeford with the exception to my man Scooby, who bought two to three ounces from time to time. My logic was if I didn't sell to anyone in Raeford, the police there couldn't get anyone to set me up. I started dealing with Scooby, because he reminded me of myself in the fact, that he was young and about his business. From this point on, I really just started playing middleman. If someone wanted to buy any drugs, I would basically called the migos, and tell them to meet me with whatever the person wanted. Then I would call my cousins and have them count out the money that I needed to make the purchase and meet me at a specific location. Then I would meet the migo, get the drugs and have whoever was getting them meet me a few blocks up. There we would handle our business, then I would call my cousins back, have them to meet in the same location as before and give them the money and have them go home and court it and call me with the count. Sometimes it would be a little short, and I would just call whoever and tell him that the money was short and he would say aight, I'll straighten it on the next go round. But most of the time, they already knew it be short. I would then tell my cousins to count how many one- dollar bills were in the bag and give me a count.

Whatever it was, I would tell them to take half and save the other half for me. I mean it would usually be around seven or eight hundred dollars. That's how I would pay them for playing their part. It's sad that when I got locked up they took everything I had. When I got arrested they pretended to be scared to have all that money in the house and wanted to move it to another location. After moving it, several times it finally ended up at my uncle's house on Jones Hill. At this point, they conspired with a guy from the neighborhood to break in and steal my safe. I was mad at first, but the Lord spoke to me and said "if I could make that much money serving the devil imagine how much you can make serving me." At that point. I was no longer upset. Now, I'm not going to sit here and lie and say that it's not times were I sit and think about what I could do if I had all that money, but at end of the day it wouldn't have done me any good. Honestly, I would have never found Christ. So, I let bygones be bygones and keep it moving. I count all my loss but dung. What does it profit a man to gain the world and lose his soul?

For More information:

Micheal Monroe

Motivational Speaking

Engagements

Email Us at kingdombiz23@gmail.com